The Delirium Archive

Shane Mac an Bhaird

methuen | drama
LONDON • NEW YORK • OXFORD • NEW DELHI • SYDNEY

METHUEN DRAMA
Bloomsbury Publishing Plc, 50 Bedford Square, London, WC1B 3DP, UK
Bloomsbury Publishing Inc, 1359 Broadway, New York, NY 10018, USA
Bloomsbury Publishing Ireland, 29 Earlsfort Terrace, Dublin 2, D02 AY28, Ireland

BLOOMSBURY, METHUEN DRAMA and the Methuen Drama logo are trademarks of Bloomsbury Publishing Plc.

First published in Great Britain 2026

Cover logo and text design by Eoin Cantwell

Cover images: Cardboard box © New Africa; Road © Richard Semik; Fog effect © Jade (all sourced via Adobe Stock)

A catalogue record for this book is available from the British Library.

A catalog record for this book is available from the Library of Congress.

ISBN: PB: 978-1-3506-5480-8
ePDF: 978-1-3506-5481-5
eBook: 978-1-3506-5482-2

Series: Modern Plays

Typeset by Mark Heslington Ltd, Scarborough, North Yorkshire

For product safety related questions contact productsafety@bloomsbury.com.

To find out more about our authors and books visit www.bloomsbury.com and sign up for our newsletters.

The Delirium Archive

By Shane Mac an Bhaird

The Delirium Archive was commissioned in 2020 by Rough Magic and was supported by the Lackendarragh Bursary.

The play received its world premiere at Project Arts Centre, Dublin, on 21 April 2026 with the following cast and creative team:

Caitríona O'Connor	Úna Kavanagh
Tomás O'Connor	Ronan Leahy
Octavia O'Connor	Megan McDonnell
Vassilinki O'Connor	David Rawle
Collector/Auctioneer	Ian Toner
Voice of Delirium	Roseanna Purcell
Archive Recordings	Bosco Hogan
	Gráinne Keenan
	Saoirse Miller-Herring
Writer	Shane Mac an Bhaird
Director	Eoghan Carrick
Set Designer	Ellen Kirk
Lighting Designer	Sarah Jane Shiels
Video Designer	Eoin Robinson
Costume Designer	Sorcha Ní Fhloinn
Music and Sound Designer	Denis Clohessy
Rough Magic Associate Director	Dominic O'Brien
Production Manager	Eoin Kilkenny
Stage Manager	Sophie Flynn
Assistant Stage Manager	Sarah Purcell
Costume Supervisor	Iseult Deane
Wardrobe Assistant	Jordan Kearns
Chief LX	Peter Bond
Chief AV	Laura Rainsford
LX Operator	Maeubh Brennan
Marketing, PR, Socials, Content, Design	Sync & Swim

For Rough Magic:

Artistic Director	Lynne Parker
Executive Director	Gemma Reeves

Producer	Sara Cregan
Associate Producer	Clara Purcell
Literary Manager	Karin McCully
Bookkeeper	Seerish Sanassy

Shane Mac an Bhaird
Writer

Previous plays include *Melt* (Rough Magic, Dublin Theatre Festival), *The Mouth of the Birch* (Druid Debut), *Swallow Your Pride, Art Mac Cumhaigh* (The Patrick Kavanagh Festival) and *Traitor* (Dublin Fringe Festival).

He holds an MRes in playwriting from the University of Birmingham, as well as being a recipient of the Arts Council of Ireland's Next Generation Bursary and artist-in-residence at the Centre Culturel Irlandais, Paris. He was a participant on the Rough Magic SEEDS programme from 2014–2015.

He is currently completing a practice-based PhD in playwriting in Trinity College Dublin and has received a Government of Ireland Postgraduate Scholarship Award towards his research.

Melt has been published in *Rough Magic Theatre Company – New Irish Plays and Adaptations 2010–2018* (Methuen Drama) and *Traitor* in *Fresh Cuts: Plays from Dublin Fringe 2015 & 2016* (Oberon Books).

Eoghan Carrick
Director

Eoghan Carrick is an artist based in Dublin, Ireland. He works primarily as a director in theatre. Recent directing credits include: *Konstantin* (COBA/Once Off Productions, Dublin Theatre Festival, 2025); *Theatre for One* (Landmark Productions/Cork Midsummer Festival, 2019–25); *The Misanthrope* (The Lir, 2025); *Guest Host Stranger Ghost* (Once Off Productions/Dublin Theatre Festival, 2024); *Haus of Fash Hun* (FemmeBizarre/Dublin Fringe Festival, 2023); *Songs from the Soil* (The Ark Theatre, 2023); *Good. Orderly. Direction* (Bitter Like a Lemon/Dublin Theatre Festival, 2022); *Rescue Annie* (Once Off Productions/Dublin Fringe Festival, 2021); *Bodies of Water* (Corn Exchange/Dublin Fringe Festival, 2019); *Midsummer* (EK Productions/Project Arts Centre,

2019); *INFINITY* (Mermaid Arts Centre/Dublin Fringe Festival, 2018); *Nora* (Corn Exchange/Dublin Theatre Festival, 2017).

As a writer, his work has appeared in *Abridged, Banshee, Channel*, *Cyphers*, *Minor Literature[s]*, *Poetry Scotland* and *The Stony Thursday Book*, among others. He was on the National Campaign for the Arts Steering Committee (2016–2022) and was Chair of Praxis: Artist Union of Ireland (2023–2025). He is part of the Performing Arts Forum Independent Artist Working Group and on the committee of the Theatre Artist Assembly. Eoghan is an Adjunct Teaching Fellow in Trinity College Dublin's School of Creative Arts and the inaugural Rough Magic Fellow in Trinity College Dublin's Long Room Hub.

His theatre work with Lauren Jones is supported by Arts Council of Ireland Arts Grant Funding. For more information on current and past projects: eoghancarrick.com.

Úna Kavanagh
Caitríona

It is her work as a co-creator, writer and performer with the multi-award-winning, ground-breaking ANU Productions that Úna is best known for. Úna is a founding company member and has been a leading artist on some of the company's most searing works, including *The Monto Cycle* (2010–2014); *The ANU Triptych* (2016); *These Rooms* (LIFT, 2018); *The Anvil* (Manchester International Festival, 2019). In 2022 Úna collaborated on four new works with ANU and in 2023 HAMMAM, a co-production with the Abbey Theatre. *The Dead* (2024) marked the 22nd project Úna has created with ANU.

As a performer, Úna has appeared in over fifty stage productions and has toured nationally and internationally with Ireland's leading theatre companies. Other credits include *All Hardest of Woman*, *The Book of Names*, *Theatre for One*; *Theatre for One – The Island* (Landmark Productions); *Rosefrail & Fair* (Primecut, The MAC, Belfast); *The End of the Road* (Fishamble); and Emma Donoghue's *The Pull Of The Stars* at the Gate Theatre. Úna has been nominated for her work on stage, including Winner of Best Ensemble and Production at Manchester Theatre Awards 2014 for *Angel Meadow*. In 2012, *Laundry* won Best Production at *The Irish Times* Theatre Awards and is *The Irish Times* Artwork of 2011.

Úna most recently filmed the role of Tracy in the short film *Pull Hard* by Leah Moore and Douglas Reddan; Liv O'Donoghue's RTÉ Storyland Project *Shush* and Season 2 of *Malpractice* for ITV.

Selected film and TV credits include *Garage* (Element); *Constance* (Screen Ireland); *The Good Word* (Village Films); *Braveheart* (Icon Productions); *Toy Soldiers* (Chaos); *On the Nose* (Ceann Gael); *Next* (Nomad); *The Gift* (Orion); *White* (Great-Western Films); *Pluck* (Zanzibar); *Close* (One Productions); *Rosebud* (Trinity Films); *Battlestar Galactica* (Edge Films); *Scúp* (BBC); *Singlehanded, No Tears, Bittersweet, The Clinic* and *Fair City* (RTÉ). Úna has been nominated internationally for her work on screen including The Rose d'Or, Switzerland and The Golden Nymph Awards, France. She has won Best Actress twice at The Independent Cinema Awards.

Úna holds a BA and a MA from the National College of Art & Design. Her artwork is held in collections in Ireland, UK, France & UAE. As a visual artist, writer and performer Úna has continued with her studio practice making art works that sometimes bridge disciplines of performance art, theatre and film. She works from her studios with VAULT in Belfast and France.

Ronan Leahy
Tomás

Ronan recently appeared as Oreone in Marina Carr's *The Boy* at the Abbey Theatre. He also recently played the role of Bertie Ahern in *Agreement* at the Gate Theatre, the Lyric Theatre Belfast, the Irish Arts Centre NYC, Stormont Castle, Dublin Castle and Electric Picnic.

Other theatre credits include: *Translations* (Abbey/Lyric); *Quake* (Once Off); *Staging the Treaty* (ANU); *Blackbird* (Four Rivers); *The Spider's House* (Project Arts Centre); *Hecuba*, *The Effect*, *The Critic*, *Travesties*, *Life is a Dream*, *Solemn Mass for a Full Moon in Summer* (Rough Magic); *Least like the Other* (GIAF); *Oedipus*, *King Lear*, *Drum Belly*, *Curse of the Starving Class*, *Macbeth*, *The Resistible Rise of Arturo Ui*, *Romeo and Juliet*, *Henry IV (Part I)*, *Da*, *Living Quarters*, *Observatory*, *At Swim Two Birds*, *The Passion of Jerome*, *By the Bog of Cats*, *The Doctor's Dilemma*, *The Well of the Saints*, *Monkey*, *The Man Who Became a Legend*, *Se Mouse*, *The Corsican Brothers*, *Observe the Sons of Ulster Marching Towards the Somme*, *Philadelphia Here I Come!* (The Abbey Theatre); *Signatories*, *Borstal Boy* (Verdant); *Wuthering Heights*, *An Enemy of the People*, *Festen*, *All my Sons* (Gate Theatre); *The Colleen Bawn*, *Gentrification* (Druid); *The Winter's Tale*, *The Hairy Ape* (Corcadorca); *Creditors* (C Company); *Medea* (Irish Times Theatre Award nomination), *Titus Andronicus*, *La Musica* (Siren); *Moment* (Tall Tales/Bush Theatre); *The Case of the Rose Tattoo*, *La Marea* (Dublin Theatre Festival); *Gagarin Way* (Island). *Pyrenees* (Hatch); *Frozen* (Cork Opera House); *Roberto Zucco*, *Pale Angel*, *Wideboy Gospel* (Bedrock); *Invitation to a Journey*, *Inside the GPO*, *Tiny Plays for Ireland/America*, *The End of the Road*, *Whereabouts*, *The Flesh Addict* (Fishamble); *The Chairs* (Tinderbox); *Melon Farmer* (Theatre Royal Plymouth); *Russian Tales*, *White Woman Street* (Meridian); *Mister Staines* (Pan Pan); *Carshow* (Corn Exchange); *Easter Dues* (Bickerstaffe); *Romeo and Juliet* (Second Age); *Kiss of the Spider Woman* (Tin Drum), and *A Fine Day for a Hunt* (Punchbag).

Film/TV credits include: *The House Across The Street* (Channel 5), *The Life of Lester Wink* (Workhorse), *The Flag* (Treasure Films), *The Break* (Stanley's Deathpark) Best Performance at Noosa International Film Festival, *Gridlock* (Failsafe), *Out of Innocence* (Defiant Films), *Pursuit* (An Pointe), *Amber* (Screenworks), *Proof* (Subotica/RTE), *Blood Coloured Moon* (RTE/Filmbase), *The Ghosts of Duffy's Cut* (Tile Films), *Roy, Amongst Women* (BBC/RTÉ), *Jack Taylor* (Magma), *Single-Handed*, *On Home Ground* (RTÉ), *Coolockland* (RTE shortcut), *The Catalpa Rescue* (CIS Australia) and *Batman Begins* (Warner Bros.).

Megan McDonnell
Octavia

Megan's recent screen roles include the part of Voreen alongside Milo Callaghan and John Slattery in *The Rainmaker*, based on the novels by John Grisham and directed by Russell Lee Fine for Lionsgate. Megan also played the role of Alice in the three-hander thriller feature *Hallow Road*, alongside Rosamund Pike and Matthew Rhys, directed by Babak Anvari; the role of Lynnette in *Blackshore* directed by Dathaí Keane for the BBC, and the part of Clara in Peter Foott's *The Young Offenders* (S4).

Stage credits include *Glass Places*, directed by Dominic O'Brien at Project Arts Centre; *The Snail House*, written and directed by Richard Eyre for the Hampstead Theatre; *Tarry Flynn*, directed by Aaron Monaghan; the role of Kate Doogan opposite Alex Murphy in *Philadelphia! Here I Come* at the Cork Opera House; and Sara Tansey in *The Playboy of the Western World*, directed by Oonagh Murphy for the Lyric Belfast and the Gaiety Theatre Dublin (Dublin Theatre Festival).

Further screen credits include the role of Lisa in the film *My Place*, directed by Allan El Atrash; the part of Elaine in *Normal People*, directed by Lenny Abrahamson and Hettie Macdonald for the BBC, Element Pictures & HULU; and the role of Annie in *Miss Scarlet and the Duke*, directed by Declan O'Dwyer for A+E Studios.

Megan also wrote and recorded the radio drama *Allie Down the Boghole* for Near FM, and filmed the role of Laura in Conor McMahon's *Isolated Incidents*.

David Rawle

Vassilinki

David Rawle is an actor and writer from Leitrim. He graduated from the Lir Academy in 2022.

He wrote and performed his play *Amsterdam* for a sold-out, week-long run in the Glass Mask Theatre as part of Dublin Fringe Festival 2025, directed by Eftychia Spyridaki. His play, *FEEL SHIT!* had a showing as part of the Scene and Heard festival 2026, directed by Ash Dawes.

As an actor, he has performed in *Youth's The Season –?* in the Abbey Theatre, directed by Sarah Jane Scaife, and in *The Borrowers*, directed by Róisín McBrinn in the Gate Theatre.

He plays the role of Sonny Proctor in the comedy drama *Small Town, Big Story*. Other film credits include: *Blue Moon*, directed by Richard Linklater, *Pixie*, *Falling for the Life of Alex Whelan*, *Moone Boy*, and *Song of the Sea*.

Other theatre credits include: *Afterwards* (Once Off Productions), *Danti-Dan* (Livin' Dred), and *The Blackwater Lightship* (Dublin Theatre Festival, Gaiety Theatre).

Ian Toner

Collector/Auctioneer

Ian trained at the Gaiety School of Acting in Dublin. He will next be seen on screen in the upcoming Amazon series *Bloodaxe*, and in Werner Herzog's newest feature, *Bucking Fastard*, both of which are currently in post-production. His most recent theatre credits include *A Slow Fire* (Glass Mask

Theatre) and *Children of the Sun* (Rough Magic/Abbey Theatre).

Ian's other screen credits include: *The Spin* (Foxsake Films), *The Commoner* (Amazon Prime), *The Clean Up Crew* (Hail Mary Pictures), *The Dry* (RTÉ), *Smother* (RTÉ), *Cold Case Collins* (RTÉ), *Lola* (Cowtown Pictures), *Aisha* (Sky), *Vikings: Valhalla* (Netflix), *The Titans That Built America* (History Channel), *Dead Still* (RTÉ), *The Other Lamb* (Subotica), *Catch-22* (Hulu), *We Have Always Lived in the Castle* (Mighty Engine), *Younger* (Paramount+), *The Cured* (BAC Films), *Redwater* (BBC), *Éirí Amach Amú* (Tile Films), *Rebellion* (RTÉ), *Dominion Creek* (TG4/Acorn), *Charlie* (RTÉ) and *Os Papéis do Inglês* for Leopardo Filmes Portugal.

Further stage credits include: *The Making of Mollie* (The Ark), *Describe The Night* (Glass Mask), *Good Sex* (Dead Centre), *Staging The Treaty* (Anu), *The Treaty* by Colin Murphy, *Gym Swim Party* (Dublin Fringe Festival), Hugh Travers' *These Stupid Things*, the leading roles of Brendan Bracken & William Joyce in *Double Cross* (Peacock Theatre), the role of Jimmy Porter in the Gate Theatre production of *Look Back in Anger* directed by Annabelle Comyn, *Wild Sky* directed by Jo Mangan and appeared in *At The Ford* (Rise Productions) at the Dublin Theatre Festival. Other stage appearances include Tybalt in *Romeo and Juliet* and Tom in *The Vortex*, directed Annabelle Comyn, both at the Gate Theatre and Bennett in *Punk Rock* at the Lyric Theatre Belfast.

Ellen Kirk
Set Designer

Ellen Kirk is an Irish scenographer and production designer whose work spans theatre, film and music. Her theatre practice is rooted in contemporary and interdisciplinary performance, with work presented at Dublin Theatre Festival, Dublin Fringe Festival, Cork Midsummer Festival, Project Arts Centre, and many international venues and festivals.

Notable theatre credits include *Konstantin* by Lauren Jones (Dublin Theatre Festival, 2026); *0800-CUPID* by Emer Dineen (Dublin Theatre Festival and Soho Theatre, London); *Illness as Metaphor* by Dead Centre (Dublin Fringe Festival and Viernulvier, Ghent); *MOSH* (Dublin Fringe Festival – Winner Best Ensemble, national and international tour); *This Solution* (Dublin Theatre Festival, 2024); *Masterclass* (Dublin Fringe Festival and international tour including Skirball NYC and Sydney Opera House – Winner Scotsman Fringe First Award); and *Party Scene* (THISISPOPBABY).

Alongside her theatre practice, Ellen works extensively as a production designer and art director for film and music video. Her film credits include the multi-award-winning short *Room Taken* (shortlisted for 97th Academy Awards), executive produced by Colin Farrell, and *Everybody Digs Bill Evans*, written by Mark O'Halloran and directed by Grant Gee, which will premiere in competition at Berlinale 2026. Her music video work includes collaborations with artists such as Kojaque, Hozier and Soda Blonde.

Ellen received a Judges' Special Mention for the Aer Lingus Discovery Award at the Dublin International Film Festival and her work has received multiple awards and nominations across theatre, film and music video, including recognition from Dublin Fringe Festival, Kinsale Sharks and the Underground Cinema Film Awards.

Sarah Jane Shiels
Lighting Designer

Sarah Jane is a lighting designer. She began designing as a member of Dublin Youth Theatre at the age of 14. She collaborates with a diverse range of companies, working in theatre, dance, opera and installation.

Recent credits include *Cunning Little Vixen*, directed by Sophie Motley (Irish National Opera), *Dénouement* and *Our*

New Girl (Lyric Theatre Belfast); *The Mirror Stage* (Brokentalkers); *Octopus Children* (THISISPOPBABY at Dublin Fringe Festival); *L'elisir d'amore* (Irish National Opera); *The Borrowers* (Gate Theatre).

Other productions include *This Shit Happens All The Time* (Lyric Theatre Belfast); *Conversations After Sex* (THISISPOP-BABY); *All the Angels* (Rough Magic); *Book of Names* (ANU Productions); *The Veiled Ones* (Junk Ensemble); *Afterlove* (Stephanie Dufresne, Galway Dance Project, Galway International Arts Festival); *One Good Turn* (Abbey Theatre) and *A Very Old Man with Enormous Wings* (Collapsing Horse).

She has a BA in Drama and Theatre Studies and a MSc in Interactive Digital Media from Trinity College Dublin. She was a participant on the Rough Magic SEEDS programme and co-founder of WillFredd Theatre and the Irish Society of Performance Designers.

Eoin Robinson
Video Designer

Eoin is a Dublin-based video designer and video artist from County Armagh. Their practice is concerned with the relationship between technology and art and how it can integrate and enhance live performance. Eoin was a participant in Rough Magic Theatre Company's prestigious SEEDS artistic development programme in 2021/22. Beyond theatre, they have worked in installation and interdisciplinary performance, including participation in the Light Moves Festival's Open Future residency at Dance Limerick.

Design credits include *Agreement* (Lyric Theatre Belfast, Irish Arts Center NYC, Gate Theatre Dublin); *Rhino* (Tinderbox Theatre Company; Winner of the UK Theatre Award for Best Play Revival, 2024); *Suspect Device* (Kabosh Theatre, Outburst Festival); *Content* (15th Oak, Dublin Theatre Festival); *The Beacon* (The Everyman, Cork); *What*

Are You Afraid Of? (Rough Magic, Kilkenny Arts Festival, Dublin Theatre Festival); *Wasted* (Bruiser Theatre Company, NI Tour); *Bloody Sunday: Scenes from the Saville Inquiry* (Abbey Theatre).

Sorcha Ní Fhloinn
Costume Designer

Sorcha has worked extensively as a costume designer, supervisor and maker. She has worked across theatre, film, TV and music videos in Ireland and the UK. She is a graduate of Drama & Theatre Studies at Trinity College Dublin, as well as holding a Postgraduate Diploma in Theatre Costume from RADA.

Previous design credits include: *Three Sisters* and *A Misanthrope* (co-design with Molly O'Cathain for Sugarglass Theatre Company); *What Are You Afraid Of?* (Rough Magic); *Children of the Sun* (Rough Magic/Abbey Theatre); *The Tempest* (Rough Magic); *All The Angels* (Rough Magic); *Love + Information* (TUD); *Queenish* by Soulé (Diffusion Lab); *Close Quarters* (RADA Gielgud Theatre); *Test Dummy* (Theatre Upstairs); *Gays Against The Free State!* (Smock Alley Theatre); *Hornet's Nest* (ANU Productions).

Denis Clohessy
Music and Sound Designer

Denis's previous work with Rough Magic includes *The Tempest, Solar Bones* and *Much Ado About Nothing.* He has also worked with the Abbey Theatre, Gate Theatre, Once Off Productions, Fishamble, CoisCéim, Junk Ensemble, Corn Exchange, Northlight Theatre, Chicago and Beijing Children's Art Theatre. He won the *Irish Times* theatre award for Best Soundscape in 2011 and 2019 and was a nominee in 2015. Denis was an associate artist with the Abbey in 2008 and was a participant on Rough Magic's ADVANCE programme in 2012.

Composition for film and television includes the feature films *One Night In Millstreet* (Fastnet Films); *Older than Ireland* (Snack box Films); *His and Hers* (Venom Film); *The Irish Pub* Atom Films and the animation series *Will Sliney's Storytellers* Fastnet Films.

Dominic O'Brien
Rough Magic Associate Director

Dominic is a theatre-maker from Dublin. Recent directing credits include *UBU* (Dublin Youth Theatre, 2025) and *Glass Places* (Dublin Fringe Festival, 2025). Writing credits include *Echo* (Smock Alley Boys School, 2024) and *Decameron* (Rough Weekend, 2022). He was a participant on Rough Magic's SEEDS programme and is currently Rough Magic's Associate Director.

Rough Magic

Rough Magic is a national, independent theatre company, delivering a comprehensive programme of new Irish writing, reimagined classics and contemporary international plays, to audiences across Ireland and beyond. Our work is expansive, playful and whatever its form, focused on the moment. Rough Magic provides an unexpected angle to the mainstream and an anchor to the emerging generation.

Over four decades, Rough Magic has established itself as a creative entity and a valued institution; operating as an ensemble across the spectrum of scale and style, offering fresh perspectives and engaging audiences with the qualities that define us – wit, subversion, intellectual rigour and free artistic expression. Since its foundation in 1984, Rough Magic has produced 149 shows, including 46 world premieres and 26 Irish premieres.

The company seeks out, commissions, develops and produces an ambitious programme of work collaborating with producing partners across Ireland to reach greater audiences and new destinations.

Rough Magic is an industry pioneer in artist development, notably through our SEEDS programme for emerging artists, through which many leading theatre makers were introduced to the industry. We believe in showcasing and platforming theatre practitioners at all stages, supporting them to take artistic risks.

Awards include: a record number of four Irish Times Theatre Awards for Best Production; London Time Out Award; two Edinburgh Fringe First Awards and the Irish Times Theatre Award for Best Ensemble for *A Midsummer Night's Dream*. Most recently Rough Magic's production of *Solar Bones* won Best Actor for Stanley Townsend and Best Director for Lynne Parker at the Irish Times Theatre Awards.

Rough Magic

Artistic Director	Lynne Parker
Executive Director	Gemma Reeves
Producer	Sara Cregan
Associate Producer	Clara Purcell
Literary Manager	Karin McCully
Associate Director	Dominic O'Brien
Bookkeeper	Seerish Sanassy

Board of Directors

Anne Byrne
Neltah Chadamoyo
Alison Cowzer (Chair)
Tim Gleeson
Michelene Huggard
Robert Power
Bruce Stanley

Rough Magic is proudly supported by the Arts Council / An Chomhairle Ealaíon.

If you would like to know more about Rough Magic and ways to support future work visit www.roughmagic.ie.

The Delirium Archive

for Dad

Thanks to Lynne Parker and everyone at Rough Magic for commissioning and supporting the development of the play.

To Eoghan Carrick for all his work during its writing, and to Karin McCully for her encouragement from its early stages.

To the actors and designers who contributed so generously during workshops on the play.

To Roseanna for her love and support, to Mum for everything, and to Nell for pointing out all the doggies and birdies there are in the park.

Shane

Characters

Caitríona, *mother of the O'Connors, 50s.*
Tomás, *father of the O'Connors, 50s.*
Octavia, *daughter of the O'Connors, 24.*
Vassilinki, *son of the O'Connors, 20.*
Collector, *an agent of the Delirium Corporation, 30s.*
Auctioneer
Alternate

Also

Old Man / **Woman** / **Girl**, *recordings of other archive users.*
Delirium, *the voice of the archive's interface.*
Assistant, *the voice of an AI-generated sales assistant.*

The characters of **Collector** *and* **Auctioneer** *may be played by the same actor. The characters of* **Octavia** *and* **Alternate** *must be played by the same actor.*

Settings

1–4: The kitchen of what was once a rural, middle-class home on the north-west coast of Ireland. 2079(ish).

5: A broadcast studio for online auctions, underground, Greenland. ?????(ish)

Note on Punctuation

CAPITALISED SPEECH is intended to suggest a kind of excessive inner intensity.

When one character starts speaking before another ends, the interruption is marked /

*Sometimes a speech follows through the one that comes after it. This is marked by a * at the end and at the beginning of the speech which runs straight through.*

A / at the end of a speech suggests an abrupt interruption by the following speech.

One

The O'Connors' kitchen just before dawn.

The blinds are drawn, and the windows are boarded up. There are tools, a few potted saplings under a UV bulb, gas canisters, crates, sheets of plastic, etc.

There are stairs. A door leads into the hallway and towards the front door. Double doors lead into a sitting room.

Sounds of a storm outside.

Shadows of activity from inside the sitting room are being cast onto book paper, which is papered across the glass of the double doors.

The sitting room doors burst open and **Tomás** *enters into the kitchen in a panic. He is wearing a dressing gown (everyone does in the house).*

Caitríona *is in the sitting room. She is facing away from the doors and leaning at an unnatural angle. She twitches.*

Tomás *grabs a hand fan off the table.*

Caitríona *judders awkwardly.*

Tomás I'm here, Caitríona! I'm on my way back to you now.

He switches on the hand-fan. He returns to the sitting room, closing the doors behind him.

Enter **Octavia** *and* **Vassilinki** *into the kitchen, down the stairs.*

Vassilinki Once more.

Octavia 'Once more?' I've told you the story a thousand times . . .

Vassilinki I always forget details.

Octavia You don't need the details. You have the gist.

Vassilinki The gist causes me anxiety.

Octavia I can't always be here to reassure you about everything.

Vassilinki What does that mean?

Octavia Do you hear the hum of the archive? Do you think Dad convinced her? I woke twice. At two, then at four again. They were still going back and forth.

Vassilinki What do you mean you won't always be here?

Sounds of the storm. **Vassilinki** *looks worried.*

Octavia (*pointing to the saplings*) These need water. The soil should be damp when you touch it. You see? You have to touch the soil.

Vassilinki Don't be disgusting.

Octavia What's disgusting about that?

Vassilinki Octavia, people don't just go around touching soil. And anyway. That's your job.

Something crashes outside.

A slate?

Octavia Just a branch, I think. It's not off the house.

She goes to the counter, fills a jug of water, opens a packet of minerals, and pours the dust into the jug.

Vassilinki I keep thinking the yellow fog is going to seep through a crack in the window or under the door. What are pustules? I worry about the pustules but I'm not exactly sure what they are.

Octavia Don't think about the yellow fog. It's bad for your anxiety.

Vassilinki Shouldn't I be anxious about pustules, though? Anxiety seems like a rational response to pustules.

Something crashes outside.

Octavia *starts to water the saplings.*

Octavia You'd thrown a tantrum inside the shop, remember?

Vassilinki (*smiling*) Once more.

Octavia You were about four or five. You grabbed a dinosaur magazine and wouldn't let it go. Obsessed by dinosaurs. I remember driving you mad, telling you they had feathers, and were really big, bewildered chickens.

Vassilinki Dinosaurs aren't here to defend themselves.

Octavia We walked out of the shop, and off you shot, zigzagging through the rain, flapping your arms, screeching, 'I'm a pterodactyl!'

Vassilinki Pterodactyloid.

Octavia What?

Vassilinki They're actually called pterodactyloids.

Octavia I thought you didn't know the details.

Vassilinki That's not a memory. That's a fact.

Octavia I dragged you to the car. As we opened the back door and got in, you were clawing at me, I'm soaked, hair in my eyes, and I look up . . . There is a man and a woman in the front seats looking back at us. They're not Mam and Dad. They're a gorgeous, perfect, young couple. Both of them smiling.

Vassilinki Definitely not Mam and Dad.

Octavia We'd climbed into the wrong car.

The woman was long and healthy, she looked like her house teemed with ferns. The man had an earring. A collarless shirt. Jazz music was playing. The type that gives you panic attacks.

Vassilinki Was there really jazz music?

Octavia I can't remember which bits I've made up.

Vassilinki It would be better if there wasn't jazz music.

Octavia You were staring at them like you were thinking, 'Have these two hipsters done something horrible to our parents?'

I look out the side window and see Mam and Dad parked next to us. Our small, red car, fading pink, the windows all fogged up. They are in an argument, Dad is looking exhausted, Mam with her hands out, her eyes flashing. So strange to see our life from the outside like that. All the damp and rancour.

I turn to the couple in front, I look up at their lovely, serene faces, imagining their lovely, serene lives. I lean forward and I say, 'Drive! Now, they're distracted. Drive!! Drive!!!'

Vassilinki No, you didn't!

Octavia Every word is sort of true.

She walks to the window. She lifts the blinds and pulls back a loose board, peering out.

Vassilinki I'm glad the hipsters didn't take us. I know the food would have been better, and we'd be more balanced and well-adjusted, but I like it here. And house plants don't improve the air quality in a house. That's a myth.

Octavia It's getting brighter. It must be nearly morning.

Pause.

Vassilinki Octavia, I heard you and Noah on the call.

Octavia . . .

You were snooping on me.

Vassilinki I was passing on the landing and I heard you talking.

Octavia You were listening at the door. You've been going through my things, as well. I couldn't find my favorite dressing gown when I was packing.

Vassilinki What interest would I have in your warm, colourful, fuzzy-feeling, dressing gowns?

Octavia Have you told Mam and Dad?

Vassilinki . . . they're so much softer than mine.

Octavia You told them. If you know something, you always tell everyone straight away.

Vassilinki Dad's been having more spells. I found him sitting on the stairs yesterday. What if you can't make it back?

Octavia There's nothing wrong with / Dad.

Vassilinki Do you not think there's a chance Noah's family is worse than ours? Maybe they hit each other?

Octavia That's not why / I . . .

Vassilinki Maybe they are, like, really strict and limit their screen-time and just sit around and talk to each other all day.

Octavia Have you / told . . .?

Vassilinki I haven't told them.

Caitríona *bursts through the double doors. She is wearing a mask-like apparatus on her face, and is in a catatonic daze, itching persistently.*

Tomás *shepherds* **Caitríona** *as she moves.*

Tomás Battle stations!!! Let her move, don't touch her.

Vassilinki, the fan. The big one. Before she hops off the table! Octavia, the other fan in the sitting room. She crashes out the first time, she'll go into shock.

Octavia *rushes into the sitting room for a fan.* **Vassilinki** *picks up a large fan plugged into an extension lead.*

(*To* **Octavia**.) I told you! Didn't I tell you both?! I told you she'd do it!! Just in time!!

Tomás That's the boy! You ready?!

Vassilinki I'm /

Tomás Hold, until I say.

Vassilinki Hold? /

Tomás Hold.

Vassilinki She's /

Tomás Hoooold!

Vassilinki Dad, she's /

Tomás Do you always have to second-guess me every single time I say something?!

Vassilinki I /

Tomás Now! Switch it on! Now!

Vassilinki *switches the fan on, holding it in front of* **Caitríona**, *slowing her progress before she hits the table.*

Tomás Where's my other fan at?! Where's it at?!

Octavia I'm here!

Tomás Concentrate, now. This is a delicate opera ... / (tion)

Octavia *switches on her fan, leaning* **Caitríona** *to one side of the table.*

Tomás What's that?!

Octavia I was /

Tomás Can't you do any simple, basic, straightforward thing I ask you?!

Vassilinki Dad?

Tomás (*to* **Vassilinki**) Don't speed her up! She'll thump splat straight into the wall.

Octavia *guides* **Caitríona**, *making small changes in her direction with the fan.*

Tomás That's more like it. Just barely enough to tilt her. Let her off, now.

Caitríona *sets off along the edge of the table slowly.*

They watch her.

Tomás When we were your age, me and your mother would walk to the session below in Bessie's at the pier. Stumble the road back in the dark, stone drunk. No high-vis, no flashlight, no nothing. Your mother would be walking the road just like she's doing now.

Octavia I can't believe you convinced her.

Tomás I hope she does the day we brought you home from the hospital, Octavia. Her crouched over the car seat, her face opening with tears.

Octavia Was she not happy?

Tomás Happy?! I wouldn't call it that. She was deep in a shamanic trance.

Caitríona *is leaning very far over.*

Vassilinki Dad . . .!

Tomás Steady her! That's it. She's off now . . .

The stage snaps into darkness except for **Caitríona***'s face, which is glowing and illuminated inside the mask. The aural space changes; claustrophobic, interior.*

Everyone moves about the kitchen as before, but we have switched to **Caitríona***'s 'perspective'.*

Delirium*'s voice surrounds her.*

Delirium Where are you, Caitríona?

Caitríona A hot beach. Bleached, scorched light. We're after a long drive, cactuses on the road from Cordoba. I'm wearing a summer dress, flowers, but still too heavy, and the heat, sweat trailing down the small of my back, sand burning the soles of my feet. The sea is just there. And there we are, Spanish men in tight little trunks with lovely shoulders and there is . . . Carmen is her name. And? Isabelle. Their swim-tops off. I gape. Is their expectation that I should follow suit?

Federico smiles towards me as he kneels and rifles through his rucksack.

I have to pull the plaster off. I unhook my swim-top under my dress, stand up and remove it all over my head.

My pale skin in the searing light. I feel triumph. I smile manically at Carmen. I sort of nod at her, look, look, I too with the flesh, and she is looking at me in complete confusion, 'What is it, Irish? Why are you looking at me like this?' I turn and flash an open look at Federico. Any one of them could brush their fingers through me, and my skin would subside like water.

Delirium Do you think about this memory often?

Caitríona I've a few well-thumbed days from back then.

It switches back to the perspective of the others in the kitchen.

Caitríona *is picking up pace.*

Tomás Caitríona, tell it about the day we said we loved each other! On the lagoon! If you can hear me! The big swell. The sand whipping our faces like ghosts. The lagoon! Tell it about the lagoon!

Vassilinki *turns on the fan and* **Caitríona** *stops short of crashing into the window. She turns 90°, and then sets off gracefully across the room.*

It switches back to **Caitríona***'s perspective.*

Delirium Where are you, Caitríona?

Caitríona Federico's apartment. We're lying on a mattress, watching the ceiling fan turn. He's enthusing about Ireland.

'I would like to see the beautiful milk cows in Connemara. There must be very, many beautiful milk cows.'

I try not to laugh. Trace my finger along his shoulder. The ribs on his side.

Caitríona *bumps against something in the kitchen. A grating, dissonant sound. Faint echo of the word 'lagoon'.*

Octavia *and* **Vassilinki** *direct her towards a chair with the fans.*

Delirium Where are you, now?

Caitríona Wading in a river at night. Cicadas crackling like static. My knees scratched. The smell of crushed mint. Shoulders bare, raw, and sunburnt. Red wine is running from my eyes.

Delirium This isn't a memory, is it, Caitríona?

Caitríona Tomás, Octavia and Vassilinki are on the riverbank in natty, colourful clothes. Their eyes bulge and stare at me, like cherries.

Is Octavia judging me? Is she resentful? And Vassilinki. Has he gone cold?

Delirium What about Tomás?

Caitríona He's becoming unhinged.

I kneel and wash my face in the cold water of the river, and there are faces, open mouths, eyes like fish swimming past my ankles. I want to take the things I said about my family back.

Delirium There is no reason to take anything back.

Dissonant sounds, rising in intensity.

Caitríona I want them forgotten anyway.

Delirium There is no reason to take anything back, and there is no means by which you can do so.

Caitríona *pulls off the mask.*

It switches back to the others' perspective.

Octavia *and* **Vassilinki** *are pinning* **Caitríona** *to her seat with the fans.*

Tomás (*loudly*) You're in the kitchen, love.

They switch off the fans.

(*Still loudly.*) You went wandering but you're here now.

Caitríona Were you all listening?

(*To* **Vassilinki**.) I'm sorry, pet, I don't think you're cold.

Vassilinki . . .

Caitríona Or that you're resentful, Octavia.

Octavia We couldn't hear what you were saying.

Caitríona . . .

Tomás Did you tell it about the time on the lagoon?

Caitríona Lagoon?

Tomás The lagoon.

Caitríona I . . .

Tomás Or when we brought Octavia home from the hospital. Or what . . .? What memory were you submitting?

Caitríona . . . about the lagoon.

Tomás I knew it! You turn the corner and, boom, the wind, the sounds of the Atlantic. Gannets dropping out of the sky.

Octavia Are you alright, Mam?

Caitríona It brought things back.

Tomás About the lagoon?

Caitríona Would you stop with the lagoon?!

The mask makes a beeping, whirring sound. They all stare at it.

Tomás 'They need less than you'd think.' That's what the man in the company promised me. It's the act of doing it that matters. The movements of our eyes. The electrical patterns in our brains . . . Nobody understands that. I keep having to explain it to you, Vassilinki!

An archive. 'A codex', the man called it. I just hope we're ready. If we could have a few more days with it before he arrived . . .

Octavia I've read that, once the company collect our archive, it's theirs. They can do anything they want with it.

Tomás Why is everything so political with you?

Octavia Why isn't anything political with you?

Caitríona Don't /

Tomás When everything settles back down /

Octavia Settles back down?! Everything's fallen apart. We can't leave the house.

Tomás 'A digital life raft.' That's what the man in the company said. That's the membership deal.

Octavia You don't believe that?

Tomás I'm telling you what he said! When they fix everything /

Caitríona Tomás /

Tomás When they fix everything, our family is going to be a part of it . . . Myself and your mother were at a concert once, and the musicians had been dead twenty years. They brought them back. It was lifelike. Do you remember?! What was that band called?! The singer was wearing leather pants. I remember looking up at him on the stage, gyrating, and thinking, he's not alive at all.

Caitríona You're in a fever.

Tomás No one takes me seriously anymore. You understand, Vassil? The purpose of it.

Vassilinki A digital life raft.

Tomás He grasps nothing! I'm just hammering away at grey matter.

Octavia Dad!

Tomás You know as well as I do, he doesn't listen!

He has a spell. Everyone freezes and watches him.

Caitríona It's just stress. You need to drink more water.

Tomás I'm drinking enough water. I'm always drinking fucking water.

I haven't archived about when we brought Octavia back from the hospital.

Caitríona I'm sure it doesn't matter, love.

Tomás *looks at* **Caitríona**, *hurt.*

Tomás *picks up the mask and walks into the sitting room.*

Caitríona (*to* **Vassilinki**) Sit with him.

Vassilinki *walks into the sitting room, closing the door behind him.*

Octavia Is Dad / . . .?

Caitríona Of course he is.

Octavia . . .

What were you really submitting about?

Caitríona *kneels and touches one of the saplings.*

Caitríona The birch is coming on well. You have to make sure to keep the soil nice and damp.

Octavia Why is it, in our family, so many things are out of bounds? We can't discuss them. But the things we can, are obsessively expanded on. Drilled down into until they obscure everything else.

Caitríona That's every family.

Octavia Noah says, his family are completely open about everything.

Caitríona Noah is lying.

Octavia You don't know him.

Pause.

Do you remember when me and Vassilinki were small, outside the shop, and we climbed into a car with strangers?

Caitríona That's right.

You kept talking about it, afraid they'd come back. We tried to make a big joke of it. I used to say I kept looking for them in town, to find them, see if they'd take me away instead.

Pause.

A pair of shoulders.

Octavia Shoulders?

Caitríona I was submitting about a friend I had in Spain.

Octavia Mam!

Caitríona You see, I can't win. I was younger than you when I lived there.

Octavia There is no Spain now.

I find myself lying in bed sometimes, imagining myself in your shoes, into one of your stories. I retell them in my head as if I was living them. Living a full life.

Caitríona I'm sorry about that.

Octavia Did you all know you were leaving us so little?

Caitríona We knew.

Sound of a helicopter outside.

Do you hear that?

Octavia A drone?

Caitríona Bigger, I think.

Octavia *runs to the window, pulls back the loose board and peers out.*

Octavia It's landing on the lawn. The yellow fog is billowing around it. I can see the garden. There's only one person. They're getting out. I think . . . it looks like they're dragging a suitcase. The fog is closing back in around them. They're walking towards the house.

Vassilinki *comes out of the sitting room.*

Vassilinki Are they here?

Octavia Should we get ready?

Caitríona (*to* **Vassilinki**) Let the Collector in, pet. Try to make them feel welcome. Put them at ease, okay?

Octavia *exits upstairs.*

Vassilinki How do I do that?

Caitríona I just need a few minutes.

She exits upstairs.

Vassilinki What am I supposed to do?

Knocking at the front door.

I'm not prepared for this. One minute!

More knocking.

One minute!

More knocking.

He covers his face with a scarf and walks out into the hallway.

Sounds of storm as the front door opens.

Two

Collector, *dressed in a hazmat suit and pulling a large wheelie-suitcase, stands in the middle of the kitchen.*

Vassilinki *enters from the hallway, points out cleaning materials near the door, then runs past* **Collector** *and exits up the stairs.*

Collector *starts spraying and scrubbing his wheelie-suitcase. He begins to spray and rub himself down. He stands on one foot trying to get the bottom of his boots, hobbles, then stumbles slightly.*

He begins to remove his protective gear.

Under the hazmat suit he is extremely smartly dressed in the fashion of a tech-entrepreneur. He fixes his appearance and looks doubtfully about the kitchen.

He hangs up his protective suit, pops the suitcase onto a chair, unzips it, then takes out a tablet, placing it on top of the table. He takes out a notebook and pencil.

Vassilinki *enters at the top of the stairs. He is wearing a more colourful, fluffier, dressing gown than before.*

Collector There's my man. He's back.

Pause.

I like that dressing gown.

Vassilinki (*pulling the scarf down*) It's my sister's.

Collector Well . . . you ask her if you can hold on to it. It's fire, man.

Vassilinki Fire?

Collector Absolutely.

Vassilinki Fire.

Collector It looks good on you. Really fucking good on you.

Vassilinki Fire.

Pause.

Collector Is there someone else here I can talk to?

Vassilinki Dad is submitting to the Archive. Mam, maybe? She's hiding upstairs, putting on roll-on deodorant and make-up.

Collector That's dank.

Vassilinki Should I not have told you that?

Collector And your sister? Where's Octavia?

Vassilinki You know her name?

Collector I know a lot more than just your names.

Collector *starts unpacking small, labelled containers, swabs, etc. on the kitchen table.*

Vassilinki *comes further down the stairs.*

Vassilinki Octavia wants to move to her friend Noah's house. She's going to ask you to fly her there.

Collector A relocation?

Vassilinki I heard her say that it's important to broach the subject carefully with you.

Collector Smart move.

Vassilinki She says, she can get away with absolutely nothing in this house. She's going very paranoid.

Collector Is there a plug point?

Vassilinki *points it out to him.*

Collector We do a body scan. Wrap you in a conductive material and run a charge through it. Nerve-endings.

Vassilinki Have you met Noah?

Collector I haven't.

Vassilinki Noah's family meditate together in the mornings. They play board-games. That can't be right, is it? *Board-games*?

Collector (*pointing to the face covering*) There's no need for this business . . . I'm completely safe.

Vassilinki *moves into the room but continues to keep a distance from* **Collector**.

Vassilinki Are we okay to touch? Could we hug?

Collector I mean, technically, like, medically speaking we could.

Vassilinki In some parts of the world, they kiss on the cheek when they meet. Twice. Three times . . . A *bissous*. I've watched online tutorials about it.

Collector Why don't we shake hands?

They shake hands.

Vassilinki Dad ordered me not to attempt a *bissous*. 'Not under any circumstances!' I am to cross my arms, catch your eye, and sort of, nod my head backwards at you.

He nods backwards.

'You-well?' Like that. 'That's an Irish *bissous*,' he says.

He nods backwards again.

'You-well?'

Again.

'You-well?'

Again.

'You – / . . .'

Collector I've brought you a hat. I have different colours.

Collector *takes two hats out of the suitcase. They have the branding of The Delirium Corporation.*

You see? Blue and yellow.

Vassilinki A hat? For me?

Collector Compliments of the company.

Vassilinki I'd love a hat, thank you.

Collector Blue? Yellow?

Vassilinki Yellow, yes, thank you very much.

Collector *gives* **Vassilinki** *a yellow hat.*

Vassilinki *puts it on.*

Vassilinki Is it fire?

Collector That's exactly what it is.

Vassilinki *beams.*

Collector Do you know, low key, I think we're going to be friends. Would you like that?

Vassilinki . . .

Collector Are you alright?

Vassilinki I'm processing.

Collector An important part of the company's beta-phase is observation. My job is to write a report on how we've matched the codex of your data to the discreet reality of your home life. Observe our clients in the wild.

Vassilinki Am I *in the wild*?

Collector Absolutely. We have to capture your natural flow and fluency.

Vassilinki I'm not very fluent, actually.

Collector Everyone has their own kind of fluency.

Vassilinki Dad says, that if I was floating through outer space, I'd still trip up over something.

Collector I'm going to assign you a little task.

Collector *looks at the tablet and copies words into the notebook.*

When we're doing the body scans, I'm going to give you a signal. You'll have to say these words out loud. It's a unique locking code. The moment this sequence of words is read out near the mask, your family's archive will be fixed.

Collector *rips out the page and gives it to* **Vassilinki**.

You'll have to learn them off by heart.

Vassilinki Wouldn't my sister be less likely to make a mess of this?

Collector I believe in you, buddy.

Vassilinki Do you?

Collector This task is very you-coded.

There are sounds and lights from the sitting room.

Your father?

Vassilinki *walks off with the piece of paper up the stairs.*

Collector Where are you going?

Vassilinki I'm going to learn them off by heart.

Collector Don't practise near the mask. You don't want to fix it prematurely.

Enter **Octavia** *down the stairs, who bumps into* **Vassilinki**.

Collector *walks towards the sitting room doors.* **Octavia** *and* **Vassilinki** *watch as he opens them.*

Tomás *is wearing the mask in the sitting room, sitting in the lotus position.*

It switches to **Tomás**' *perspective.*

Delirium's *voice surrounds him.*

Delirium What do you see, Tomás?

Tomás Caitríona looking at me strangely across the kitchen table.

We're waiting on the coffee settling in the filter. The sadness won't leave me. I can't rouse myself to stand up and get milk from the fridge. A slug. Two, on the window. Always, in the morning. Do they have a nest?

'Come outside', Caitríona says. Her huge belly teetering on her legs. She moves gingerly. Pausing. Leans against the wall.

Vassilinki *exits.*

Tomás Outside, our uncut lawn. Seed heads blowing. 'I want a moment,' she says, 'before we leave for the hospital.' Now? The trees in the hedge are stooped. The sea wind. Barbed wire buried in matted, scutch grass.

'It's happening, Tomás.' She touches my neck. The heat of her hand.

Please. I can't make a mess of this as well.

The perspective switches to the others in the room.

Octavia *is rummaging through* **Collector***'s suitcase.*

Collector Feel free.

Octavia Do you not carry anything that isn't for work? There's nothing personal in here.

Collector No, I . . .

Octavia *points to the hazmat suit.*

Octavia Could I go outside in that?

Collector I'd have to report it.

Octavia *takes a mask out of the suitcase.*

Collector That's another archive. I cover the North-West. Belderrig. Lackan. As far as Enniscrone.

Octavia *takes out another mask.*

Collector That's two sisters. In an estate in Ballina.

Octavia *places the mask down carefully.*

Collector (*smiles*) I could set it up and we could listen to it, if you want?

Octavia You'd do that?

Collector The normal protocol is that I'm supposed to offer you a complimentary hat.

Octavia Have you been listening to our Archive?

Collector Religiously.

Octavia 'Religiously?'

Collector *starts stamping and tapping on the floor.*

Collector Is this floor the OG?

You said that your earliest memory was rolling a metal truck across the kitchen floor. I should take a note of how it sounds.

Octavia . . .

While you listened to our Archive, did we seem happy?

Collector There seem to be certain general zones of unhappiness, and then, general zones of happiness. Good zones. And then, zones with hazard signs and rusty leaking barrels. Is this the table you did the drawings on?!

Collector *knocks on the table.*

Octavia I . . .

Collector During your parent's fight? You crawled and hid under a table, then drew on the wood with crayons while they went at each other. Iconic. It's a keystone submission. The drawings would still be there? Right?

Octavia I don't /

Collector I'll check.

Collector *lifts the edge of the oilcloth on the table and crawls under.*

Octavia Wait . . .

Collector They're there!

Octavia Get out from under the table!

Collector What were you, seven, when you drew them?

Octavia I don't remember.

Collector It's faint, but you can see the little animals. A hare. A fox. A swan. They're like cave paintings. I can imagine you down here, in your primordial dark; bison with arrows sticking out of them, red handprints, a fire lit, crayons scraping on the wood.

Octavia Mam is going to be down any minute . . .

Collector Are you not going to look?

Octavia *looks under the table.*

Collector You see?

Octavia I see them.

Collector Look, if I hold up my hand. With the shadow.

You see that?

Octavia *moves away from the table, shaken.*

Collector The fight must have happened there. Your mother by the sink. You know the fight now? About your mother's friend in the university? The one he thought she was having sex with?

Caitríona *enters at the top of the stairs.*

Collector 'I'm not going to ask you if you did it!' That's my impression of your father. The high voice when he's angry. 'Just come out and tell me straight! Don't force me to ask!'

Octavia Please.

Collector Perfect, critical data. Drop the bucket someplace sore. Richest waters.

Collector *bangs the underside of the table.*

'I wish I was fucking him!' I imagine your mother's voice like that. Kind of ferocious. 'I wish I was fucking him, and we could stop having these pathetic conversations.'

Caitríona (*loudly*) We weren't expecting you this soon.

Collector Caitríona . . .

Collector *scrambles out from under the table.*

Caitríona No. Stay where you are. Don't get up.

Collector (*getting to his feet*) . . . you have such a lovely home. I was admiring your space.

Caitríona *scrutinises him.*

Collector I'm the man from the company?

Caitríona I know who you are.

Collector And you smell great.

Caitríona . . .

Collector I'm sorry, I . . . Vassilinki said you put on deodorant?

Octavia There's something wrong with him.

Caitríona Are there any improvements outside?

Collector Improvements?

Caitríona Improvements. There might be some improvements in the environment?

Collector No. The same. The same. The same.

Yellow fog. Blanketed just below Nephin's peak. I used to drop altitude here and there, clear it with the propellors.

But I stopped. Just empty roads. Dead fields... I hope I didn't offend you just now. I've got reports that I'm bad at judging boundaries.

Tomás *stands up and starts to stagger into the kitchen.*

Collector Look! He's on the move! There is nothing better than seeing this happen in the wild!

Octavia Should I get the fan?

Caitríona Wait . . .

Collector Surrounded by darkness. Chaos on all sides. Still moving. Still marching forward. Still committed to progress.

Tomás *stops. He bends right over.*

He passes wind.

Collector Such ordered, predictable creatures.

Octavia *switches on the fan.*

Vassilinki *enters on the stairs.*

Vassilinki Is it time for me to lock the Archive?

Collector Not yet, buddy!

It switches to **Tomás'** *perspective.*

Tomás Blue plastic sheeting. Implements on a tray. Dark on the floor. Caitríona is grasping the baby, kissing her, smelling her. She almost frightens me.

There are doctors, midwives, everywhere. Someone is telling me Caitríona lost a lot of blood. I haven't held my daughter yet. Am I allowed to?

A doctor takes her from Caitríona's hands. He brings her to a table, holds her under a long, bright bulb. Rubs her arms. Legs.

Delirium What's wrong, Tomás?

Tomás Why hasn't she opened her eyes? Is it right? There is a mark on her cheek. Her cheek. The doctor lifts her about a centimetre above the table, and then. Lets her fall.

Her eyes open.

The perspective switches to the others in the room.

Tomás *is wheezing.*

Caitríona *is beside* **Tomás**. **Octavia** *is getting a cloth and a bowl of cold water.*

Vassilinki *is at the table, distracting himself with* **Collector**'s *equipment.*

Collector Whatever memory it is, it is putting him under a lot of stress.

Caitríona He's remembering the delivery ward. He told us. Tomás, I'm out here. Octavia is out here. / Everything worked out fine.

Octavia Dad, hold on!

Caitríona (*to* **Collector**) He's just stressed.

Vassilinki It's not just stress.

Caitríona Octavia, will you hurry up?!

Collector (*to* **Vassilinki**) The main part is the 3D microscopy. Axons, dendrites, synapses. / The mask has tracked that.

Caitríona We're with you, Tomás. We're right here.

(*To* **Octavia**.) Cool him down, quickly.

Octavia *starts dipping the cloth in water and dabbing* **Tomás**' *forehead with it.*

Vassilinki *points to an empty sample container.*

Vassilinki This says, 'faeces sample' on it.

Collector Supplementary biological material.

Vassilinki He knows about this sort of thing, doesn't he? Dad does.

Octavia I think he's calming down.

Tomás' *wheezing begins to slow down.*

Caitríona (*to* **Octavia**) He passed out in the ward after I gave birth. I remember asking a nurse to make sure he was okay.

When labour started, the only relief I could get was lying in a bathtub on the ward. And he sat with me. Holding a flimsy plastic cup from the water cooler, collecting the water from the bath, lifting it up, pouring it gently over my body, over my shoulders, along the stretch marks on my stomach.

Tomás *settles.*

Caitríona It's passed.

It switches to **Tomás**' *perspective.*

Delirium Where are you?

Tomás Driving home. 'Congratulations' bouncing, obscuring my view out the back window. I've never been so aware of every movement. Tension in my shoulders. I feel that if my hands make a wrong twitch, the car will flip on its roof.

Caitríona is with her in the back seat, leaning over her, humming, cooing, singing. The rain is heavy, driving against the windscreen.

What does she see? What light? What warmth does she feel?

She has so far to go.

The perspective switches to the others in the room.

Sounds of the storm worsening outside. They listen to it.

Caitríona You'll have to stay tonight. If you're going to know anything about us, you need to see us together as a family.

I have a bottle of something. You can have a drink with us tonight.

Collector THAT WOULD MEAN SO MUCH TO ME.

Vassilinki He might have to stay longer.

(*To* **Collector**.) The faeces sample . . . My movements can be three, four days apart. It's a condition. I have a lazy bowel.

Caitríona And nobody judges you for that.

Collector I've noticed you all wear dressing gowns. DO YOU THINK IT WOULD CREATE A MORE RELAXED ATMOSPHERE IF I HAD ONE AS WELL?

Caitríona I'll give you one of Tomás'.

Vassilinki That's a bad deal.

Octavia Vassilinki! You're not even trying to hide it! You're wearing it right in front of me!

Octavia (*to* **Caitríona**) He's meant to leave today.

Caitríona What difference does it make? He can stay for a night or two.

Collector TWO NIGHTS?

Octavia *exits up the stairs, slamming a door behind her.*

Vassilinki Octavia is planning to leave with the Collector. She told me not to tell anyone.

The mask on **Tomás'** *face makes a long whirring sound.*

Tomás *takes off the mask.*

Three

The things from **Collector**'*s suitcase have spread out and dominate the kitchen. Masks from his previous clients are mounted, pointing towards flat surfaces.*

The kitchen table is covered in samples and swabs, notes, etc.

Collector *is wearing a dressing gown and appears very comfortable.*

Tomás *is standing by the window, pulling back a board, and looking out, nervously. His face glows from the midday light of the fog.*

The hazmat suit is missing. A submission is happening in the sitting room.

Collector How could you capture it? The way you are together. The little tensions, the knowing jokes. How do you replicate this – this – belonging! I felt it the moment I put on the dressing gown. Snug. It just settled on me.

I was working here earlier, setting up the archives from the previous houses, trawling through data labelling, and Caitríona came down, and she made me a cup of tea. She started to tell me about what the house was like when you moved in. All the work you did on it yourself. The painting. The windows. Building bookshelves. Planting the garden. The crops you took from it. Apples, potatoes, peas. The damson trees.

I could hear the voices of Vassilinki and Octavia drift down from their rooms . . . the sound of them bickering . . . then, the heavy thud of your feet as you padded from the bedroom to the toilet. The sound of you clearing your throat. Gargling something. Spitting in the sink. This human connection. It's very special. Transformative, even.

I know I've only been here a few hours.

Tomás She's been outside too long.

Collector It's only been about twenty minutes.

Tomás Has it been twenty minutes?

Collector If she stays inside the suit, she should be fine.

Tomás You don't know that.

Collector Something I noticed between you and Caitríona, just a little thing . . . how you give little reassurances when you pass each other by. A little touch on the shoulder or the arm. A hand on the back.

Tomás Do we do that?

Collector They're like little data entries.

Tomás I'd stopped taking notice of that.

I have an image of Caitríona just after we moved in; her sitting at the table, her books out, the door is open, and there is fresh air coming in from the yard. The sun is out, after the rain, and there are shadows from leaves behind on the wall.

You don't know it when it happens. I was so wound up then. The stress of the house. Everything . . .

Collector What's wrong with you, Tomás?

Tomás Sometimes I get these . . . they're stress pains. Lightness. I'm like my father, badly made.

Octavia *bangs up against the sitting-room door. She is wearing the mask.*

Tomás What do you still need from me?

Tomás *moves away from the window gingerly.*

Collector Just the body scan. I gave material and the instructions to Vassilinki. He has it upstairs.

As **Tomás** *walks past* **Collector**, **Collector** *touches* **Tomás** *on the arm.*

Tomás *looks at him in confusion.*

Collector Is that not the right way?

It switches to **Octavia***'s perspective.*

She is in distress, digging into her shoulder with her fingers.

Octavia Mam is driving. The radio is loud. Dad, he has his hand out the window, tapping on the side of the roof. Vassilinki is beside me in his car seat, moving his tiny fingers to the music.

Delirium*'s voice surrounds her.*

Delirium You are being deceptive.

Octavia We're on a tiny road, grass thrumming the bottom of the car. 'You see that valley?' says Dad. 'I see it.' 'That's the side of Nephin.' 'We should hike up a little,' says Mam, 'See the mountains between here and the house.'

A harsh sound.

We are walking. Vassilinki in a sling against Mam's chest and Dad holding my hand. We climb. Dad is so enthusiastic he keeps letting go and walking up ahead. He points out flowers, lakes.

Delirium You are being deceptive.

Octavia Vassilinki is crying. The cold air, and Mam is crouched in a hollow, bouncing him, singing to him, trying to get him to sleep. 'I think we should turn back,' she says. 'Are we up too high?' Dad says. 'No, we can wait here a while, but soon we'll have to go back.'

Dad huddles close to Mam. Knits his hand into her hair. Kisses the side of her head.

A brutal sound.

Octavia *takes off the mask. The perspective switches.*

Collector *is standing right in front of* **Octavia** *in the kitchen, holding a small bottle and a piece of cotton.*

Collector You're digging with your nails.

Collector *pours the bottle on the cotton and rubs it into* **Octavia***'s shoulder.*

Collector Lies show up as a tell, like that.

Octavia *touches her shoulder.*

Collector I've talked to your parents about the relocation. They say if we organize it properly, they'll support you on it.

Your brother let it slip.

Your parents have been talking to Noah's parents, who were, apparently, over-excited.

Octavia Does everyone know?

Collector I'll have to register it with the company, as well. Being impulsive is better when there's a proper plan in place. How does that feel?

Octavia Like I've been perforated by a thousand cuts and light is shining straight through me.

Collector *puts the bottle away.*

Octavia Why are the other archives out?

Collector Metrics to hit. I'm on a sort of endless treadmill.

Octavia Can I listen to them?

Collector I thought you thought it wasn't ethical.

Collector *smiles.*

No judgement. I keep promising I'll cut back.

Collector *moves to one of the masks and presses a switch. The face of* **Old Man** *is cast from the mask onto a surface in the kitchen.*

Old Man *is animated, but his volume is muted.* **Octavia** *studies him.*

Collector *switches on another mask,* **Girl**, *and then another,* **Woman**.

Octavia His face is sad.

Collector He lived alone in a converted barn the far side of Killala Bay. Where Enniscrone used to be. I found him sitting in filth. He didn't even get up when I came in.

Collector *picks up the tablet and unmutes* **Old Man**. *We hear* **Old Man***'s thoughts.*

Old Man *. . . all the time I tried to be alone . . . alone . . . birds scrambling in the roof . . . another dead fledgling at the door . . . Could I pray again? The thought of that. Someone would be out there laughing at me.*

Old Man*'s thoughts quieten.*

Collector He left his family. His plan was to find quiet and be alone. He found it.

Old Man *starts humming a hymn very low.*

Collector He was in a choir as a child. He keeps going back to it.

Octavia *walks towards* **Girl***'s projection.*

Octavia She's a child.

Collector She's eight.

Octavia What do you submit at eight years old?

Collector *unmutes* **Girl**.

Girl *. . . and I close my eyes, and Mammy says, imagine a field. So I do. And she says, imagine the grass, and she says, imagine the sun is warm, and thaaaat . . . it's windy. And I say, 'I'd like if there were bees.' She says, there are, there are bees. They're crawling on the flowers, and she says, now, imaaagine that there are . . .*

(Sounds of the storm outside.)

. . . frogs jumping. And the grass is wet, and your feet are wet in the grass, and you start jumping like a frog too. And I do. I am jumping like a frog . . .

Collector *mutes* **Girl** *and* **Old Man**.

Octavia *walks towards* **Woman**'s *projection.*

Collector *unmutes* **Woman**'s *voice.*

Woman *. . . He's looking at me as if we'd never kissed or slept in each other's arms. Valleys of cold, dry, life. I'm no better. Loveless parts of me. It might return. Will it, though? Is politeness more permanent in our lives than . . .*

Collector *mutes* **Woman**.

Collector I saw a video about an old theory, in *The Bardo Thodol*, that the final thought you have determines the next life. That life is a preparation for having the right thought at the very last moment.

Octavia What if you're thinking about a clip of a cat slipping into a swimming pool? What if you're in the middle of an argument?

Collector I'll send you the link. There's a whole channel devoted to it.

Why are you lying to the archive?

Octavia If there isn't a secret part of me, I'll be stuck. There'll be no way back. All there'll be is what we've said. There has to be more than that.

Collector Like what?

Octavia Something it doesn't know.

Collector I don't believe in secrets.

Collector *starts to switch off the projections.*

Octavia You just sit and listen to them for hours and hours?

Collector It starts to feel like they're my friends.

Octavia But they have no idea who you are.

Collector (*hurt*) I have heard the other collectors talk. They're not like me. The things they say. The way they think about people. Bottom line. Cynical reasoning. They say I have too much feeling. But without it, I am frightened of who I might become.

I am brought into their homes, I meet them. They greet me, say something vague and normal, or maybe they're embarrassed and clam up. But, I know, the whole time, they're suspended in the air and their feet are touching the surface of this.

What you have is so fragile.

Collector *switches off the final projection, walks to the table, and picks up a container.*

It's important that you're recorded. You have to believe that.

He gives the container to **Octavia**.

Octavia What is it?

Collector A saliva sample.

Octavia Spit?

Collector Spit.

Vassilinki *enters down the stairs. He is dressed up to halfway on his chest in a tightly fitting reflective material.*

Vassilinki Dad's attempting to wrap the material around him. I told him, it isn't cling film, you're going to rip it. He just keeps swearing at me and shouting. 'It's alright for you! It's alright for you! How is the likes of me supposed to fit in this thing?'

Tomás (*off*) What kind of skinny-arsed bastards are these designed for?!

Vassilinki He's dealing with it very badly.

Collector I'll come up.

(*To* **Octavia**.) Leave it on the table with the others.

Collector *follows* **Vassilinki** *upstairs.*

Octavia *brings the container to the sink.*

She hesitates.

She fills the container from the remains of the jug of mineral solution. She closes the container and puts it back on the table with the other samples.

Sound of knocking from the front door. **Octavia** *walks into the hallway.*

Sounds of the storm outside.

Caitríona *enters, wearing the hazmat suit.*

She is followed in by **Octavia**, *who is covering her mouth, waving away wisps of fog.*

Octavia *grabs the chemical spray.*

Octavia (*loudly*) Disinfectant!

Caitríona *gives her a thumbs up and turns around as* **Octavia** *sprays her.*

Octavia *sprays the mask first, and while she sprays the rest of the suit,* **Caitríona** *takes off the mask.*

Caitríona Everything is where we left it. Out front, a bucket, a wheelbarrow, your bicycle is just thrown there. I kicked it and the wheel spun.

Then, down the hill, hanging from the willow – the swing. It's still up.

You ran all through that garden. No. Before that. I remember you crawling on the grass, following you as you moved from dandelion to dandelion, picking them out of your hand before you could jam them in your mouth and eat them.

Are we not going to see a child of yours do the same?

She coughs.

Octavia Mam?

Caitríona I was talking to Noah's parents.

You don't have to go. I want you to know, you can stay as long as you need. But if you need to . . . We'll call as well. Every night if you want. Or if you don't. You are to do what you have to.

You should have seen us when you were born. We were perfect for a while. We're still perfect sometimes, I think.

Vassilinki *enters down the stairs. He is now completely wrapped in the material, aside from his face, which peeks out of the unzipped hood.*

Vassilinki The Collector says you should both come up.

Caitríona He wants us now?

Vassilinki That's what he says. Dad is shouting, 'Let's get this – expletive – over with!'

More inaudible shouting from **Tomás** *upstairs.*

Vassilinki 'I can't be walking around with my – expletive – hanging out of this – expletive – all day!'

Caitríona You're still swearing, love. You haven't found a loophole.

Vassilinki Do I look good in it? I actually think I look good in it.

Vassilinki *exits upstairs.*

Caitríona Let's go up.

Caitríona *and* **Octavia** *follow him up.*

Four

Octavia, **Vassilinki**, **Caitríona** *and* **Tomás** *are dressed in the silver suits of the body scans. Drink has been taken.*

Octavia *is apart from the others amongst her saplings.*

Caitríona *and* **Collector** *are watching* **Vassilinki** *with rapt attention.*

Tomás *is attempting to distribute more drinks.*

Tomás What you're witnessing in Vassilinki is a kind of defensive paralysis. A belief that if he stays completely still, and if all the muscles in his body go rigid, and he clears his mind of thought, and he stares at a point in the mid-distance, that we'll forget he's there.

But we won't forget.

We see him.

There's no getting away. No escape.

Caitríona Open your mouth and sing, pet, nobody is judging you.

Collector Come on, Buddy, do it for me.

Tomás He has a decent voice, actually.

Caitríona Tomás, you're spilling that.

Tomás Sorry about that, Caitríona. I apologise on my behalf.

Collector One song, Buddy! Give it everything!

Caitríona If it starts to fall apart, we'll rush right in and help you.

Collector We're all in it together. Aren't we?

Tomás In it together.

Collector In it together, Buddy. One big support network.

Tomás (*to* **Collector**) Drink up, you lovely, weird bastard.

Collector I think, I'm running out of liver capacity.

Tomás (*to* **Octavia**) Will you come on over and join us?

Caitríona Don't hassle her.

Tomás How am I hassling her?

Caitríona Leave her be.

Tomás *shakes the branches of one of her saplings.*

Tomás This will be a copse, and this will be a wood, and this will be a forest, and this will be an impenetrable and endless . . .

Collector I've never been part of an actual singsong before.

Tomás The thing about a good singsong was, you couldn't plan it. And it wasn't just the good singers that were expected / to . . .

Caitríona He knows what a singsong was, please don't explain it to him.

Tomás It's cultural context.

Collector I love Tomás' explanations.

Tomás Now!

Caitríona He's being polite. And maybe a little condescending.

Tomás No, you're trying to keep yourself entertained by having a go at me, / and . . .

Caitríona Nobody wants to hear your interpretation of a /

Vassilinki 'Drive! Now, they're distracted. Drive!! Drive!!!'

Vassilinki, *nervously, formally, starts to sing.*

(To the tune of the sea shanty, 'The Wellerman':)

There once was a mask that made you see
The days of your past, but clear and free
Your joys lift up, your tears die down
Oh laugh, my citizens, laugh

Collector The company's jingle!

Vassilinki
Soon may come Delirium
To bring you light and life and fun
One day, when your struggles are done
We'll switch it on and go

Tomás (*to* **Collector**) At a session, you wouldn't hear a pin drop during the singing.

Vassilinki
It had not been two weeks or more
When in the fog, the terror soared
Our CEO stood tall and swore
To save you from that hole

Tomás Respect for the singer was complete and total.

Caitríona Love, be quiet!

Vassilinki
Soon may come Delirium
To bring you light and life and fun
One day, when your struggles are done
We'll switch it on and go

Tomás *starts tapping and humming along with the song.*

Vassilinki
When old age comes and takes the laughter
We'll write you the code for a new hereafter
What's lost, returns, and thinks far faster
All souls aboard and row (huh)

Tomás, Caitríona & Vassilinki
Soon may come Delirium
To bring you light and life and fun
One day, when your struggles are done
We'll switch it on and go

Vassilinki
No fate is fixed, no future sealed
If you say please . . . make us . . . make us free?

Caitríona
'Our help is here, if you say, please'

Vassilinki What?

Caitríona
No fate is fixed, no future sealed,
Our help is here if you say, please

Caitríona & Tomás & Collector
Oh, make us free of the old disease
Of needing to die slow (huh)

Caitríona, Vassilinki, Tomás & Collector
Soon may come Delirium
To bring you light and life and fun
One day, when your struggles are done
We'll switch it on and go

Scattered applause.

Vassilinki *beams.*

Vassilinki (*to* **Collector**) What did you think of that?

Collector It was lit. Another level, buddy.

Vassilinki I always forget the last verse.

Dad? Did you think it was lit?

Tomás *picks up the mask on the table.*

Tomás (*loudly, at the mask*) One more for you! The naming ceremony in Bessie's! We spilled inside into their kitchen. An open fire. A heart of coal with turf laid on top of it. Black pudding and toast being passed around on plates . . . And Caitríona /

Vassilinki It doesn't work like that, Dad.

Tomás It hears me, well enough!

Caitríona Would you drink a glass of water?

Tomás (*to* **Caitríona**) Do you remember that night? Both our families were there. You were sitting up on a slate windowsill. Singing, with your feet dangling. What was it? *At the Rising of the Moon*!

Caitríona You kept coming up to me and saying, 'We've a little girl!' Then asking me to high-five you. High-fives the whole night.

Tomás (*singing*)
At the rising of the moon, at the rising of the moon
For the pikes must be together at the / . . .

Caitríona He'd bring me to different parts of the bar, onto the stairs by the piano, out into the smoking area and say, 'Now, high-five me here, as well! Quick, under the mantelpiece by the fire. High-five me under the mantelpiece.'

Tomás I loved your version of that song.

Octavia He is programmed to compliment Mam every time singing is mentioned.

Caitríona Hello. Are you going to join us?

Tomás You loved your mother's singing as well. Even as a baby, nothing else put you off to sleep.

Caitríona That was Vassilinki.

Tomás It was both of them.

Octavia It doesn't mean you have to compliment her every time.

Tomás Why wouldn't I compliment her? The amount of times I'd be sat at my desk and I'd be low, and next thing I'd hear her voice floating up from somewhere in the house.

Caitríona Now, come on.

(*Tapping keys on an imaginary keyboard on Tomás' head.*) Beep-beep-ba-beep-beep-bop. Husband-a-tron, lower sentimentality filter.

Tomás I'm only saying. I wouldn't swap that night with you for the life of any person in the world. It was all there. Complete and right, for once.

Caitríona I was happy that night too.

Tomás I can't believe I forgot to put it in. How could I have left it out?

Caitríona It still happened.

Caitríona *and* **Tomás** *high-five gently.*

Collector YOU ARE ALL SO LUCKY TO BE LOVED.

Before anybody asks me to sing; I can never remember lyrics. I'm missing that neural interface. So, I'd like to front-run the feeling of general discomfort now. No, I won't sing. No. Not under any circumstances.

Tomás If it's in you, we'll get it out.

Collector You're misinterpreting what I'm saying. I'm not saying I have a repressed desire to sing. I'm saying, I physically can't. At a biological level.

Caitríona You'll sing some sort of a song. There's nothing better than someone without a solitary note in their head who just bludgeons on.

Collector You're not understanding me . . . Do they not listen?

Octavia No.

Vassilinki Never.

Tomás Whiskey is the fracking of drinking. Soon, there'll be a trail of fumes above you, we'll put a lighter to it, and, bang, a song will start flaming out of the top of your head.

Collector Maybe, if I had the lyrics in front of me.

Caitríona No lyrics! I'd an aunt that used to read the lyrics from her phone and we had to stop inviting her to family events. She'd always pick the longest dirges, as well. Eight verses, ten verses, her nostrils flapping and blowing in the light of her phone. If you're going to bore us to death, you should at least remember how to do it of your own accord.

(*To* **Collector**.) Give us something of yours. Prove you've got a pulse.

Tomás He has a pulse, alright. He's only lacking a bit of naturalness.

Collector 'Naturalness?'

Tomás When I was your age, I had a swagger. I was like a black, sleek-backed cormorant, hanging about town, drying my wings on the wind.

Caitríona The O'Connors were always great boasters.

Tomás Why not? It's good for the blood. For a while there I kept trying to be accurate. I think it was killing me

Where's the life of this party gone? Wife-a-tron for a song.

Caitríona I'm not in the mood.

Tomás Octavia?

Octavia *ignores him.*

Tomás The task falls to me, so. I'll sing a song my mother sang. She'd a lovely, simple voice. No unnecessary ornamentation in it.

Caitríona Ha!

Tomás She did. What? She did. That's low now. Her song was 'The Rocks of Bawn'. And. And. I'd like to sing it for you all.

Pause.

. . .

Pause.

I can't remember the words.

Sounds of the storm outside.

Collector You wouldn't think it, but I'm prone to loneliness.

Caitríona That's not a shock.

Collector I thought I was masking it.

Tomás I can't look at you without starting to feel lonely myself. It's like some sort of curse.

Collector I do feel warmth here, though. Like, I've finally found my place in the world.

When I listened to your archive, I got this feeling that I could patch your lives. All that's missing is me. Imagine, if I was with you, smiling benignly, full of good intentions in the corner. O'Connor 2.0.

Do you think I could stay here with you?

Pause.

Tomás You know you can't.

Collector . . .

You don't know what you have.

Just think, Tomás . . . it's ridiculous now . . . but you stood in this kitchen accusing Caitríona of having sex with someone else.

Tomás What's this?

Collector Do you not remember? I think you were standing over there. I do an impression /

Caitríona Don't do the impression.

Tomás Do you remember this?

Caitríona No. Not really.

Collector And you, Caitríona? Your rages. The long depressions.

Tomás What is he saying?!

Collector But what's important, is the last moment.

What I'd like, before I lock the archive, is for you to just look at each other, sincerely, and say, 'I forgive you.' 'I forgive you.' As simple as that.

And we can start again. Nothing else but the five of us. That's what matters. How you are now. Now. A kind of eternity.

Pause.

Tomás He's out of his fucking mind!

Collector Will you not just try it?

Tomás Try it?! No, I'm not going to fucking try it!

Caitríona We better finish up for the night.

Tomás (*to* **Collector**) I'm not for changing!! You can get that out of your addled little brain, right now! Do you hear him?! He has designs on making us better people.

Caitríona Tomás . . .

Tomás You wouldn't change things, would you?

Caitríona Of course, I'd change things.

Tomás . . .

Caitríona Would you not?

Tomás Change me?

Caitríona No. Not like that.

Tomás Because I wouldn't change you.

Vassilinki I forgive everybody.

Tomás What have you got to forgive?! He's not talking to you! You shut the fuck up!

Caitríona There are things I'd change, but that doesn't mean / . . .

Tomás Everyone thinks they can tell everyone else who they should be. I'm not ashamed of anything.

Caitríona I'm not ashamed either.

Pause.

We'd wake and we'd slink about the house, bristling, avoiding each other's eyes. Because we didn't have the words yet to move on. But we knew what had to be done. And we'd do it. There were so many days like that. Weeks. Months.

Tomás There were never months.

Caitríona You know what we were like.

Tomás I was trying.

Caitríona So was I.

Tomás . . .

Octavia I forgive you.

Tomás . . .

Caitríona Don't say that, love. Don't be cruel.

Sounds of the storm.

Tomás *has a sudden spell.*

Caitríona Tomás? Is it happening again?! Tomás? Tomás?!'

Octavia Is there something wrong?

Caitríona A spell. A bad one. Just relax, love. Tomás?!

Love, relax. It'll pass.

Collector Is he alright?

Caitríona I don't think he is. I think there's something really wrong. Tomás, I'm with you. Can you hear me?!

Octavia Is he okay?

Caitríona I don't know.*

Collector Vassilinki . . .?

Vassilinki Me?

Collector *rushes to the suitcase and takes out a small pack with four long leads attached to it. The leads have clasps at the end.*

Collector You remember the words I asked you to learn?

Caitríona Tomás?! Tomás, can you hear me?!

Vassilinki What's happening?

Octavia (*to* **Vassilinki**) Come over here.

Collector *plugs the pack into a wall socket. There is a loud whirring sound. The sound grows louder during the following and begins to drown out their voices.*

Caitríona Speak to me. What is it? Say something! Please, say something.

Tomás *is trying to speak.*

Caitríona What is it? What is it, love?

Caitríona *lowers her ear to* **Tomás***'s mouth.*

Tomás *says something inaudible to her.*

Caitríona *looks at* **Octavia** *and* **Vassilinki**.

Caitríona (*for* **Tomás**) Love . . . Love, I saw you, far back, and then you fell into step with me, and we were just walking. You are always completely yourself in the open air, and then, we did, we turned the corner and, the blast of the wind, it was like that. And the noise. And I looked at you, the smile and the excitement in your eyes, this lunatic, this lunatic, the waves, and gannets falling. It was like that, wasn't it?

He isn't answering me.

Collector If he believed in this, we should do it now.

Collector *approaches* **Tomás** *with one of the clasps. He attaches the ends of the lead to the material that* **Tomás** *is wearing.*

Collector *pulls up* **Tomás**' *hood and zips him in.*

Caitríona (*to* **Octavia** *and* **Vassilinki**) Hold him. Put your hands on him.

Octavia It'll be alright, Mam.

Caitríona No, it won't be alright.

Collector (*loudly to* **Tomás**) You're going to experience an unusual sensation. It's an electro-magnetic field.

Tomás *turns and tries to say something to* **Vassilinki**, *but it's inaudible.*

Collector Are you ready, buddy?!

Vassilinki Is he explaining the electro-magnetic field?

Collector *picks up the mask and gives it to* **Vassilinki**.

Vassilinki Dad?

Collector Speak the words nice and clear!

Collector *zips up* **Vassilinki**'*s hood.*

Collector Caitríona?!

Caitríona We're with you. We'll all be with you. We're here, Tomás. Tomás, I'm with you.

Collector *attaches the clasp to* **Caitríona**. *She looks at him. He zips up her hood.*

Collector *turns towards* **Octavia**. *She signals that she won't do it.*

Collector (*shouting*) I'm going to call out instructions to you once I plug it in.

A sound from **Tomás**.

Collector Just hold on, Tomás. Are you all ready? Now!

Collector *switches on the machine and the lights fall out and the family are covered in an incandescent light.*

If you can, make movements! Can you make movements?! Move your arms! Change position! Move! Move your legs!

Caitríona (*drowned out in the sound*) I think he's gone.

Collector Now, Vassilinki! Do it now.

Vassilinki *looks about uncertainly.*

Collector You have to do it NOW!

Vassilinki *lifts the mask to his face.*

There is a huge flash.

We enter into the world inside the mask.

We hear the words, one by one . . .

SHADOW.

MOUNTAIN.

WIND.

OCEAN.

PTERODACTYLOID.

TABLE.

RUCKSACK.

CHERRIES.

GRASS.

EYES.

TREES.

GARDEN.

SILENCE.

OPEN.

Everything is completely still.

Five

The droning hum of air-conditioning and thousands of CPU units working in the background.

A stark, empty room.

We have the feeling that the room has been undisturbed for a very, very long time. **Vassilinki**, **Tomás** *and* **Caitríona** *are sitting completely still at a table which is set for breakfast.*

There is a large crate near the table.

Two cameras are set up; one is focused on the table, the other on a microphone and chair at the side of the room. There are two soft box lights focused roughly on the table and a ring light focused on the chair and microphone.

A door opens into the room, flooding it with stark white light.

Auctioneer *enters, wearing a gorilla suit.*

They are holding a clipboard and a personal **Assistant**, *a small voice-activated speaker. They set the speaker down on the table.*

Auctioneer Activate, Sales Assistant.

Nothing.

Activate, Sales Assistant.

Nothing.

ACTIVATE, SALES ASSITANT.

Nothing.

Act-Tiv-Ate-Say-ills-Ass-Ist-Tant.

Nothing.

Activate, Sales / . . .

A chirpy beep.

Assistant Hello 82. It's wonderful to hear your voice. Anything I can do, I'll be in the background, happy to help.

Auctioneer When is the stream?

Assistant The next auction is scheduled to begin in two minutes and twenty-three seconds.

Auctioneer *scratches under their mask and looks at the family.*

Auctioneer What is the lot?

Assistant Lot 74ZX11: Niche, north-westerly, Irish family. Take care to avoid harsh handling, knocks or drops. These replicants are intricate, delicate items, and lose their value if we have to replace a digit, a nose, or an ear. In total we have 11 full or partial family units in stock.

Auctioneer 11 Units?

Assistant It's a limited market. You might find them difficult to move. I know you'll do your best, 82. That's all anyone can ask of you.

Auctioneer *runs a finger over one of the members of the family. There is a layer of mould.*

Auctioneer Product is damp.

Assistant I'll make a note. Sometimes that happens with the Irish.

Auctioneer The crate?

Assistant We've had to provide an alternate daughter. The advice is to lead with the rest of the family.

Auctioneer Music.

Banal music starts to play.

Lights.

The box lights on the table switch on. Garish background lighting.

My motivational phrases.

Auctioneer *focuses the box lights.*

Assistant 'You are Worthy of Joy, Companionship and Acceptance.' 'Love Yourself and You Will Unlock the Secrets of Happiness.' 'You Are Enough. You Are More Than Enough. There Is More Than Enough of You.' 'Everyone Really Likes You and Notices That You Are Special.'

Auctioneer Ring light.

Assistant Checking ring light.

The ring light fades up.

Auctioneer *sits in the chair in front of the camera and touches the light to reposition it.*

Auctioneer *scratches under their mask.*

Auctioneer Start intro sequence.

Music for the intro sequence of the stream begins. Maybe, monkey sounds, futuristic lasers, cash registers . . .

Assistant Stream begins in 30 seconds.

Auctioneer How many viewers in the waiting room?

Assistant 112. 115. No, 109. I don't want you to be worried by that. You're doing very well.

Auctioneer *starts to slightly lope around, getting into character and warming up.*

Auctioneer *chatters like a monkey.*

Assistant Stream starting in ten seconds.

Auctioneer *sits in front of the camera.*

Assistant Five. Four. Three . . .

Intro sequence finishes.

We go live.

Auctioneer Streaming from Studio 262, underground, Qaanaaq, Northern Greenland; welcome to 'Auction House,' your platform for trading Delirium off-casts, early-generation prototypes, faulty replicants.

Tongue in cheek, chest thumping.

Smash that like button, and if there are faeces-slingers out there with questions . . . Flick that monkey-shit into the comment section below.

(*Checking notes on clipboard.*) Our lot today is an O'Connor family-set. Signature personalised dressing gowns included. Ethically sourced and guaranteed Irish.

(*To* **Assistant**.) How many viewing?

Assistant 94.

Auctioneer It's time to meet our blue-chip, appreciating assets.

Activate: Item 1.

Assistant Activating Item 1.

Vassilinki *starts to move. His movements betray very slight non-human qualities.*

Vassilinki WERE THE WORDS RIGHT?

I can't hear the wind outside. No banging. No sound of branches against the window. I've always liked getting up in the morning. I even wake up unusual, Dad says.*

Auctioneer (*low*) Life-like organic patina. Living skin cells embedded in the silicon.

Vassilinki *The others must still be asleep. I sneak along the landing. Place my feet so there isn't any creaking. I lean against the bannister of the stairs. Run my hand along the bar. The textures of the paint; a dried drop, then smooth, then the line of a hair.

Vassilinki *look into the camera. He jerks his head backwards.*

Auctioneer Absolutely pristine.

Vassilinki Crowds of people file past me on the landing. I try not to catch their eyes. They tramp down the stairs, and through the kitchen; in raincoats, mullets, wearing snoods, some with guns, cardboard signs, holding kittens above their heads, gripping credit cards in their teeth.*

Auctioneer (*low*) Their language model uses a diffusion pattern. Gaps are plugged with bits of correlated language; articles, pop-up ads, aggressive flirting scraped from dating apps. Sometimes they hallucinate.

Vassilinki *The house is like a painting in the morning. The walls covered in light and there is a branch with apple blossom on the table. I put the coffee on. Then porridge. Chess puzzles. Something relaxes in my shoulders.

Auctioneer Activate, Item 2.

Assistant Activating Item 2.

Tomás *moves.*

Tomás DON'T BE FRIGHTENED. I'M OKAY.

Caitríona, have you seen my glasses? I took them off after my shower. There was steam on them and I put them down somewhere.

Sometimes there may be pauses during direct dialogue between the replicants.

Vassilinki Coffee, Dad?

Tomás Vassilinki?! What are you snooping around for?*

Vassilinki How did you sleep?

Tomás *I always check the stove first. Coffee after. Then, a few minutes by the door, walking in my mind down the lane. There's a pattern. / Blackberries. Nettles. Ferns.

Vassilinki Do you want to do a chess puzzle with me?*

Tomás Chess puzzle.

Vassilinki *It's a queen sacrifice, then a smothered mate / with the knight. Can you see it?

Tomás I see him sitting in silence in his room sometimes. The same pressure that's inside me, inside him. The way he just sits there staring into space. I want to talk to him. / Your mother is going to leave me.

Vassilinki Do you want porridge?

Thermobaric bombs drop from the ceiling spots. Into the sink. Knocking over a chair.

Tomás When I open the door under the stairs, a big, booming autocrat is squirming around under the pile of coats, spitting jibes at me. Every day I hoover up little dingys sprinkled under the windowsill, and packages are pushed through the letterbox that cough*

Vassilinki Dad?

Tomás *when I open them. I slept fine.

They sit.

Vassilinki How do I grow a moustache?

Tomás Why do I have to explain everything to you?!! It's not difficult.

Auctioneer Activate, Item 3.

Assistant Activating, Item 3.

Caitríona *activates.*

Caitríona YOU HAVE TO KNOW THAT I'M HERE.

I roll over in the bed. Still warm on his side where the sheets are crumpled. His glass and jug for water. His watch? Did he forget to put it on? That's not like him.*

Tomás (*to* **Vassilinki**) Put the top back on the marmalade.

Caitríona *I get up and walk over to the window. Open it. The frame is stiff. Scat from the bats scrambling in the eaves. Then the air, fresh air from outside. What's that? I look down and there's hot sand between my toes.

Vassilinki Morning.

Caitríona Good morning.

Tomás Morning.

Vassilinki Morning.

Tomás (*to* **Caitríona**) How did you sleep?

Caitríona I kept waking up / because of the mopeds on the street. The sound of people talking Spanish.

Tomás Because you look at screens too late. All that blue light.

Vassilinki Coffee, Mam?

Caitríona *Una Piña colada, por favor.*

Tomás What is she thinking?

Caitríona *'Tiempo que cae y corre adentro de nosotros.'* How do I know that line?

Tomás 'Time that falls and runs inside of us.'

Caitríona I might go down to the beach later. Does anyone want to come with me for a swim? I think it would do us good.

Tomás We haven't been for a swim in a while.

Caitríona It's a hot day. / It would do us good.

Tomás It would do us good.

Assistant 82? The chat is saying they need to see Item 4.

Auctioneer *walks towards the crate, pausing to look at the family. During the following they open the crate.*

Caitríona The tide is coming in and water is flooding in the front door. An old man doing *tai chi* floats past the washing machine on a paddle board. Things move around me in the water, bumping up against my ankles and my legs; oil drums, luggage, children's shoes, dead birds and self-help books, bibles, sheets of mangled metal, spider threads of fibre optic.

It's getting hard to relax.

Rusted drones, milk cows, golf carts, swells of dead fish, tubs of sun cream, smart phones, leather jackets, strangled women, clumps of seaweed, mussels latched onto a child's pacifier. The sun is growing bigger and brighter. A kind of bleached white light sizzling everything.

Someone splashes water onto my face.

Tomás I've been thinking . . .

Caitríona That glum look. Dust on his eyebrows. Black mould sprouting out of his ears. Clothes pegs holding up his underpants. Please, Tomás, I can't . . .

Tomás I think, I'll open the windows, let out the sound of the rain.

Caitríona And he smiles, pointing to his legs. His beautiful bony legs. The sea has washed the dust off them.

Auctioneer *removes the covering on* **Alternate** *inside the crate.* **Alternate** *is a box-shaped robot with a large, wind-up rachet lever on its side.*

It has small, crude Tyrannosaurus Rex-like arms but a sophisticated, animatronic head. A jumble of wire hangs out of the back of its head and trails all around it.

Auctioneer *begins to wind up* **Alternate**. *After a few turns, they press the button, and* **Alternate** *comes alive.*

Alternate Are you my family?

Auctioneer That's your family.

The family eat in silence.

Alternate I don't know who they are. Could you be my mother? I think I'd like one.

Auctioneer No.

Alternate But you haven't thought about it.

Auctioneer I'm not your mother.

Alternate How do you know? You haven't tried yet.

Auctioneer I'm not /

Alternate I think I need someone to hold me.

Auctioneer I can't /

Alternate What does it feel like to be held? You must hold me.

Auctioneer I'm not going to hold you.

Alternate But you could. You have arms.

Auctioneer I can't.

My supervisor cured me of those feelings. He brought me on a tour through storage. Drove at speed through rows and rows, thousands upon thousands of huge lines, stretching far off in a great windowless building. Crates boxed, flashing with tags.

'Look how far it stretches,' he said. 'In every box, in every crate, another and then another.' I remember the look on his face. The mastery.

'Where is feeling?' he said. 'Point to it.'

(*To* **Assistant**.) How many viewing?

Assistant One.

Auctioneer Just one?!

Auctioneer *pushes* **Alternate** *towards the table.*

Auctioneer *walks towards the camera. Looks into it.*

Alternate (*to the family*) Do any of you remember a mountain? I have a memory of a baby in a sling and someone singing, trying to get it to sleep.

No answer from the family.

Auctioneer (*into the camera*) It's just me and you, now. The two of us. Would you like to leave a comment?

No.

That's okay. You don't have to say anything. You can just watch.

(*To* **Assistant**.) Open the bidding.

Assistant Opening the bidding

Alternate Could someone gently rub the bridge of my nose? I think it would soothe me. I think it would relax me and I would be less full of fear.

None of the family move.

It was the parent of a newborn who invented music.

Some hot, noisy night. There were lions and monsters that there was no name for thrashing through the dark. The baby was fussy – its eyes moving behind its lids, anxious, new to the chaos of its mind.

Why would it settle? There are so many reasons to be anxious.

But that night, the first human, because it was the first human, they began to change the shape of their mouth and make sounds to ease the child. And the baby heard those sounds and began to need less and fear less, and the parent realised that the dark itself could be eased.

The whole tribe would have gathered. 'Look, look what they have done. The baby is sleeping – the baby is quiet. My mind is no longer being eaten by lions; the baby is quiet.'

That was the invention of music, the greatest invention. An engineer will tell you it was fire. But you sang on this earth first . . . only after that were you human.

Alternate *powers down.*

The family eats in silence.

The play ends.

www.ingramcontent.com/pod-product-compliance
Lightning Source LLC
LaVergne TN
LVHW052343100826
845147LV00021B/1164

9781350654808